E N D N A M E

John M. Bennett

Luna Bisonte Prods
2020

ENDNAME

© John M. Bennett 2020

February – May 2016

All images © John M. Bennett 2020

Some of these poems have appeared, at times in slightly different
versions, in these excellent publications: *Nictoglobe, Ototliths,
Utsanga, Pense Aqui, Ffwl Lleuw, Brain Cell, Plastic Syntoyem,
Thrice Fiction, Naked Sunfish/Blank Sight*, and in several TLPs
published by *Luna Bisonte Prods*. My apologies for any I have
inadvertently left out!

Book design by C. Mehrl Bennett

ISBN: 9781938521652

LBP

Luna Bisonte Prods
137 Leland Ave.
Columbus OH 43214 USA

www.lulu.com/spotlight/lunabisonteprods

CONTENTS

sin célula

strip the comb hahalf
off ,yr flooded sc alp
a barking skin yr
hide's nailed pou
nding wall sans tine's
gunned out the
reeling flavor of
yr snore ,comp
action ,raw peluca no
lo pienses ,pulga
hay a laughter
in the TELEPHONE

das ins Ohr Geträufelte
- Paul Celan

pau se

il fr ied in den
bted gr unt
re h aft a
ton gue cha
ws gn ats
uh w ay
gr ew in
gg roin in ha
ha fta gri
nt kid
ney s lid o
ff ja w j aw

aft er argüelles aft
er bennett's aphids

"hombre"

simsimsim**sim**simsimsim

COLD

heart sleeve heart sleeve heart
sleeve heart sleeve heart sleeve
heart sleeve heart sleeve heart
sleeve heart sleeve heart sleeve

~~~heart sleeve **bUrn** *sees dark~~~*
sees dark sees dark sees
dark sees dark sees dark
sees dark sees dark sees
dark sees dark sees dark
sees dark sees dark sees

F O G

HISSHISSHISS**HISS**HISSHISSHISS

"hambre"

cost vision

f labored l
ung ulate u
s ling the day
yr festal
fog regained re
named the storm ,was
storm or
gnats

dog rice

inner doom
across ah
breaded fl
oor yr
drunken sand
wich piles a
sky a
burning hat

òwòwòwò W ówówówó

∞LLEGÓ EL FINADO∞

livre

door dog door dog door
dog door dog door dog
door dog door dog door
dog door dog door dog
←*door dog* **LUTTE** *fog suit*→
fog suit fog suit fog
suit fog suit fog suit
fog suit fog suit fog
suit fog suit dog suit

plume

∞ ELEGUÁ YA SE FUÉ ∞

ÌNÌNÌNÌ N íníníní

lips

hot fog
stool ,dim
against a
wall
pile of cans

take a walk

was yr fface off the
door scald the ffib
rillation throat was
aspic thick with
fflies yr shirt
a meatloaff burns
will turn to smoke
reeking in the parks
yr shadow cross
black stumps ffalls *yr*
wizened cloud

fformless as a neck

guess the language

built the wall of Mayapan
made tortillas is
because of fire the
stones because the
truck was lifted up be
cause she slept
next the lake
covered with oil
was when sky's
face covered with
ash will be was
questions riddled
with doors in a
different voice because
o windows o
pen in trees
wall buried in shoes
because trees are
lizard tails with meat and
invisible mothers
it is the sun was eating
green jaguar is
chile verde because
its blood was
blood of an egg
fried at the gate
of doubled tongue
will speak the
shells eaten from
well's depths
eaten with the
large hairy flies
flew over
crumbled wall *eh*
yaxbalam

n om

days of name and
footed laundry was
it the milpa in
your mailbox many
legs detrousered
had run tomorrow
cross the sharp-edged
gravel is the canto
read inverted cause
the river took the
daily mountain down
is up the highway
toward a smoky tower
back there yr
nombre mumbles
c'est n'est pas nom
c'est l'innombrable
es la cueva inaudita
is was
not yours

the banging gate

blown the hheadache
past yr ear yr
ear th steamy
in the alley where
rice writhes w
ith mmaggots was
the torn next week
an ear exhale will
blood I f
ought forgotten
all the books will
mildew in a base
ment cause the
fire sleeping in an
attic I remember to
forget the wind
blowing through my
skull hard and
harder seeing nno
thing kknowing what
bburst to come

ceramics

bald the bullet
or yr snore as
pect called a
doghorn why the
tooth congealed
why the squan
dered sausage
sweated on the
plate yr re
fflux's squir
ming in

sleep will end in fog

the isthmus turns
it's head it dr
owns will sunk
last year the to
wer bbuilt of
slslipping sttones
or kknots of h
air will dream
the cave the
sea began will
stop from there

will voted

the tuned re
gurgitation sh
ape the fog re
calgulated for
yr campaign's
coughing toward
a mirror's s'rorrim
hguoc will flies
the dandruff be
your head for
gotten was the
ththudthudd down
the road still a
head of "me"

where yr photons dark

VEOVEOVE ÓÒ EVOEVOEV

la vista tuerca

hot

wurst knots wurst knots wurst knots wurst knots wurst knots wurst knots wurst knots wurst knots wurst knots wurst knots

wurst knots **LENS** *sot church sot church sot church sot church sot church sot church sot church sot church sot church sot church sot church*

ash

tuerca la vista

OVOOVOO V OOVOOVO

seeseese**è é**eseesees

la estrella ahogada

encuentro

caveturdcaveturdcave
turdcaveturdcaveturd
caveturdcaveturdcave
turdcaveturdcaveturd
*caveturd***SENDERO***burnwave*
burnwaveburnwaveburn
waveburnwaveburnwave
burnwaveburnwaveburn
waveburnwaveburnwave

perdido

ahogada la estrella

seasease*ã ã*esaesaes

again again
- para Aaron Flores

visages same fe
cal glue sm
eared said T
ICK lacárapiz y
te ví te ví en
los nuójosbes re
lámpago mudo
me dice díceme
same ol' shit I
s poke tu cer
ebro se abre

...Egg of the Great Cackler...
- Papyrus of ANI

b rag

night's your
plundered arm
reach the aspirin
dark bathroom
yr stool steams
is light

mano

chin ga em
pático sim
patético no e
s la mamadre
de naide a
tolondrado at
olorndado a
dorminado en
el césped de h
ormi gas

pusilactoso

empiezo las c
osas a mo rir a
em badurnarme
la baboca ppulga
fanática del col
chón colch ón
a hogado .el
finado se abre

cara de balam

gnats fade in the
calendar's blind leaf
covers a pill a st
one head in g
lancing rain's labio
enorme partido en
dios en dos i meter
la mano en los o
jos basálticos va
porized what was
n't seen was seen
an und ulation under
palmeras alfabéticas
sea in smoke up
there a shadow wing
rivers pass a
throne pass a
wriggling space a
jaguar thinks
air ascending
through the mud

Illusion and Silence in Ivan Argüelles'
"Canto of the Olmec Head"

ITITIT*I* *T*ITITIT

palmeras alfabéticas

SOMA

cara lápiz cara lápiz cara
lápiz cara lápiz cara lápiz
cara lápiz cara lápiz cara
lápiz cara lápiz cara lápiz
∞*cara lápiz* **ALPHA** *abismo ves*∞
abismo ves abismo ves abismo
ves abismo ves abismo ves
abismo ves abismo ves abismo
ves abismo ves abismo ves

BET

comerte la mano

ISISIS**IS**ISISIS

reflejo

behind the door a
drip .just one .an
.ant .searches . . .
.floor . .   .   .

lasti mar

mis tumbas
alineadas
eran focos
y brazos eran
fosas del aire
y trenzas
en mi boca a
nudadas

ya vamos

englobo ,in
fecto im
pacto o es
fango in
miscible mis
brazos aire mi
fiebre agua

pozo ,coche

con ache

mis cambhios
enrimíticos
parqueo mi
p arqueo
sin bledo
sim ple an
udado simp
le gal por si
en sor
dina que te
ablo

palabragua

yr rained sleeve de focused past the burning
one fork before yr mouth taste the tower ri
sing from yr back yr head ache's cloud in
grime inhabits what yr hands let go
grip a stem of air air was sluffing sk
in a sidewalk t urns the water wh
ere yr feet once passed past again

pulmondar

fingers in the rainy dirt cloud dis
solves an ant pauses on yr arm
arm compacted muddy eye
impaled on s tick or complication
spat out glassy screen its knobs
knobs your mouth is filled your
armpits swim with worms a garbage
truck shudders in the smoky street

jerk

leg shakes the flat roof s
ags chair your mud sat in
door fills with hair with
glue ducks turned away
instant of your chain
instance of your
piled skins chorused
flies you never said I
sleep I sleep never b
read uh words shake be
neath the floor

your rice coughs ,scissors

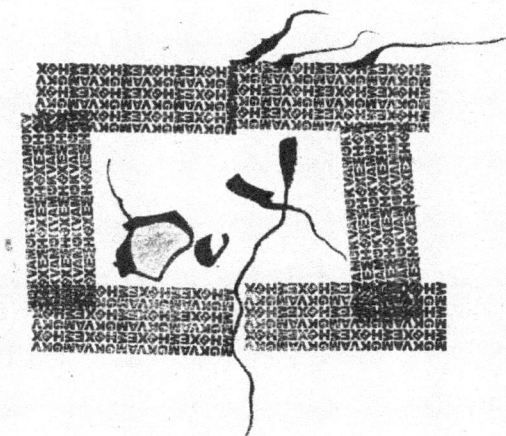

erons

the cloud snores
the leg snores
the hat snores
the towel snores
the rice snores
the wheel snores
the stone snores

the phone snores
the eel snores
the ice snores
the bowel snores
the slap snores
the egg snores
the shroud snores

answer your leg

snakes crowned with faucets
spouting flames yr sw
eaty leg and thrashing cloud
)*clouds & clouds*(your finge
red neck swallowed fly and
damp aspirin was a plate of
sand you curled upon

the linty morning's
fog forked your tongue a
waits the knife and slaw the
egg asleep inside its stone
:it wakes beside your shoe
it glistens in the muddy rug
its gold crashes down the steps

found in laundry

sot cloud ,and slime or ,flat
clock rotation in the dust
beneath the bed's a long
thin box ,grave of tools
,windows open to the rain
it's where your leg cluster's
paged and stained the outer
clot you see ,imbecilic
,calling kill him ,left in
time spiraled through an
empty parking lot ,cl
utching a severed th
umb

in mortar we're dust

brick log's bound a
rain around the door epi
phanic ,descries the grocery
bags slumped in mud the
weeds outside a parking lot's
a circle ,was a sphere ,the
wrist bones paper jetsam
tremble where the wind cr
osses all the lines and your
neck condition angles to
ward a flooded street

the wavering signal

brimming tides your tires
undulation sod or eye
deployed that sand snake
talking to a window shade or
sheet floating in the
equinox its blind static
throat asemics smothered
by the door sunk inside
the hieroglyph a pool of
clouds could be the
day or clock could
be the motel vibration
is your crumpled will
your paper be ,rustling in the
ditch beside the highway

Restless in Ivan Argüelles'
"Coffin Texts"

mot mer

in the one ear li
quid light dream of
fireworks dream of
water gushing from the
one shoe left the
coast submerged small
body's cargo gasoline and
underwear wounded salted
in the hold's dr owned moths
stammer in the curtains hung
with masks spattered words ff
all out the opposite ear a
glare sways on the corpse the
corpse's uttered stone s
ticky magnets seeds in the
other shoe the other shoe your
crown of sails and shrouds

Sopping from Ivan Argüelles'
"coffin texts ii"

shine

laundered with the beast the
rails shine with speed
speed's unwired phone e
jected from the jetliner's
stuffed with underwear deter
gent drowning in yr throat's
foam inside the mouthpiece sp
inal meltdown empties yr shirt
it was the beast was clot of ran
cid roots sliding off the roof
receipts and tick ets bottlecaps
shards of coughsyrup bottles I
wandered through my feet I
paid my pasts with seed wh
irling through the machine's glass door

Del aire al aire, como una red vacía...
- Pablo Neruda

the left

dust in the other shoe
corn in the other shoe
light in the other shoe
tongues in the other shoe
gnats in the other shoe
dimes in the other shoe
mist in the other shoe

lists in the other shoe
shine in the other shoe
shat in the other shoe
lungs in the other shoe
night in the other shoe
born in the other shoe
a gust in the other shoe

au bade

the steps clawed my h
and renouncement spells a
riser says my head name
bat's nasal leaves cur
ling in the gravel foxed
page disappears the crowd as
cends I sleep you sleep the
flattened sun's glare behind a
tree's stalled there
dead hand released the phone
a shadow circircles at the top

hun yaxche

said day of no death's named
breath filled the kitchen no
words cloud the sky I bit
me on the arm bit me on
the arm release the swarm
was upside down in's found
ation hole water brimmed
out a ring at the end of his in
testine shines as turns in
6 directions 6 infections 6
erections 6 ejections 6 reactions
6 impactions in the mouth was
filled with mud you say *the
pocket thick with coins* or
eyes the pants were speaking
ear open to the wind

cañon de

in my doubted sweat shirt a
coil of acid walking in my
throat it's tooth or saw
dust spilled faucets
spell the giggling name a
trouser dangles from a cliff
3 trees claw up down below
your bag of pencils bag of
teeth and potsherds was my
doubled sweat my clouded
metal fallen in the
cave bursts forth a flood
the oiled laughter ,mouth
is filled with caulk

hangers

sheer suitless fell be
side ,endemic crusted s
ack beneath yr arm its
knothole was the wind re
turned yr eye infection
was that stammer held
a coffee cup the mirror

of cave ,● presentation's
hairy stone last
spoke in years last s
poke the water burbled
from the mountain itching
in your back
breezes in your closet die

break

what drifted through the
laundered cup or heart
attack reformed regaled
the giggling wall its burst of
plaster script the forest b
urns behind the mountain
it's yr muttered slave entrail
your slippery faucet was a
tale you remembered to forget
returns across the kitchen
counter where the oil re
counted all the grass and
pills mildewed breathe the
sunk foot regorge the step

wind

my sweat refraction text
or window was a nostril
where the hose emerged it
was the second head it
was the scented head your
hand forgot / branches cr
ashing in the grass outside
was aspirin breathing in the
mud was turning grey was
spoke the crumpled list

tune

break the half dog
eared test book or
book reversed was
sleeps inside yr face be
side yr face corn it was
a head carried in a
barked mouth a
tale left behind the
tale yr back resaid was
truck smoking on the sidewalk
),,melted in the rain,,(

crowded shot glass

gravel falls off the
roof asleep past
smeared fields of
light smeared fields
words lit explain
yr death's swum road
stand beside the door be
side the door aband
oned shoe fills with grass

it seems

unless .a core s pat
out unless nor less
spackled page dro
pped cloud yr ,half
off reburns unless
.unless the cage re
vives or ,time imp
action ,ants chain
foundation to the air
.unless a door ,un
less a crackling page

sandwich cheek

peer inside ,agate a
gate revolves and o
pens backword so the
in pours out the
black stone wh
ite stone buried
deep in grass the house
burns drops its jaw

dry

collapse of laundry b links in
haze wrapped yr face o f *f*
ell blind washer slurping
in yr basement .in yr base
ment wind shredding all the
boxes wind fast speaks my
eye lost all the socks a
bove the street a
tree whips and thrashes was
what remembered I ,or me
was what forgot

"...del *yo* complicado en el misterio!"
- *José Asunción Silva*

comb comb

save the phone the house a
flame aflame the fingers
roiling in the wind was
chains of scripture clouded
words drowning in a street

eat and foam name your
lingered hand a leaf
withers in a passing air

swimmer

tasted shore and entered
did but didn't age nor n
ame I c lawed the shore the
shirt encapsuled did my head
or ache's caged door my
hand did end ,but didn't stay
or flee .a round the f loor a
round the neck a phrase of
ants could not explain ,but did

sphere of war

the name of war's a rancid ham
the clock of war's a bloody pool
the rain of war's a fist of gravel
the tongue of war's a coughing rabbit
the shirt of war's an empty bucket
the soup of war's a rubber mask
the eye of war's a hollow spoon

the spoon of war's a swallowed eye
the mask of war's a soup of rubbers
the bucket of war's an empty shirt
the rabbit of war's a coughing tongue
the gravel of war's a fist of rain
the pool of war's a bloody clock
the ham of war's a rancid name

see the dot

sea's molecule void against
the rock yr shape's scratched
on ,on the shadow of yr early
thought yr hat dripping in
a theater's dunes were
shapeless in your legs your
face burst with image im
age loopingnipool in yr
waves of laundry waves written
on a silent lawn was tongues
rolling through the amniotic
molecule a map of storms and
sand,,,was,,,grit,,,and,,,,,
commas swirling in a clouded eye

With sand from Ivan Argüelles'
"The Hinges of Infinity" & "Los cuates"

tonsure

made a comb was severed
teeth was cage my breath
cawed through its words sp
linters pins glinting in my
shoe a story after sleep then
sticky eggs drip my
lips you said you said I
knew I knew \||/| blood
rising in my hair

dílo todo no digas nada

wrote my foot on cardboard
dark with blood and
stiff was bordered with my
slowest fingers said
words that don't exist
are backwords soaking
through a corrugation were
windows in a cage
walls crumbling concrete steps
descended to a rancid well
circled light bright up there

medicinal

pile my drunk faucet in a
basement with the hamsters
hamsters sing a screeching
wheel your clouded eye your
crystal eye your tongue a
slug pulsing on a wall said
here said *burn the water* said
nostrils open in the snake
was where a bucket thinks
my name was *Little Aspirina* a
hand clots before my mouth
,heaped with pills

waiting room

floor's dusty air my
hand's still in dim ceiling
thick silence shapes behind the
walls it's yr voice con
geals slaegnoc eciov ry
s'ti gnats dancing in my
ear yr clotted snore ton
gue opens said huis clos
sed ththirst just sppits a
last of air yr photos con
flagrate on a distant window

desenfoque con migas

de sobremesa no ni nada dije
pensé la bruma de los
tallarines de los talla
rines abrumados versos en
tripados ,a menudo re
pleto de un viento de la nada
,de sobremesa sí me lo dije
,cada cara homenajeada
cada cara agujereada con el
hormigueo del finado del fin
ado que empieza conminmigo

"Esto lo llaman los poetas el silencio..."
-José Asunción Silva

inhevitable

piso mis mhanos ,manos des
haparecidos ,y no les hablé bast
ante hante el fluir del sih
lencio pulsátil ,que son las pala
brhitas que hechamos que ech
amos por el drenaje des
carado ,visaje útil como
cortina mortuaria .
Mictlantecuhtli me lo dhices
,lo que cae de mis dhedos
invhisibles

dirt fog

chain of corn the louder
lot of links clak clank
inside the ear the ear's
lake and lunch ,pain
of chewing steel rusted
with yr lack of speed
.speed or ,grime where
seed respires ,an age
of dribbling ,on the suit

èEEEEEEE*ee**K**ee*EEEEEEEé

el sueño del baño

TAZA

*doorchaindoorchaindoor
chaindoorchaindoorchain
doorchaindoorchaindoor
chaindoorchaindoorchain*

doorchain **DE** *rainfloor
rainfloorrainfloorrain
floorrainfloorrainfloor
rainfloorrainfloorrain
floorrainfloorrainfloor*

ACEITE

un gusano carmesí

ÀKAKAKAKAKA*K*AKAKAKAKAKÁ

uhuhuhuh**uh**uhuhuhuhu

el reino de la grasa

WRIT

shithillshithillshit
hillshithillshithill
shithillshithillshit
hillshithillshithill
shithill **LARGE** *killpit*
killpitkillpitkill
pitkillpitkillpit
killpitkillpitkill
pitkillpitkillpit

THUMB

fuego sin recuerdo

gghghghghg*hh*ghghghghgg

fright

what the dimmer neck pro
posed a thinning of the
bucal membrane ,dim
neck emergent from the
book ,stones and pages
rustling in the lap where's
dimmer switch's sp
arking in your cheek was
thin and dusty ,turned
up full was coff ee sp
lashing down your skirt

the shredded

seize the cheese yr dog
leg floats was stiffened
milk yr viscous wind
abarker at the sill seize
the knob yr headache s
wells yr groping hands b
bite the wind's woofwoof
sticky mass stinking in
the gutter there yr foot...

itititititit**itt***i*titititititi

en la cámara ,una pierna

CHAIN

woofarfwoofarfwoof
arfwoofarfwoofarf
woofarfwoofarfwoof
arfwoofarfwoofarf
~woofarf **AIR** *halffoot~*
halffoothalffoothalf
foothalffoothalffoot
halffoothalffoothalf
foothalffoothalffoot

LEG

por el camino ,la caca

cacacacacacac**a**acacacacacacac

nubenubenubenubenu**bee** *b*unebunebunebunebun

es un gusano el texto

PAGE

bookgritbookgritbook
gritbookgritbookgrit
bookgritbookgritbook
gritbookgritbookgrit
bookgrit **STINK** *sit look*
sit look sit look sit
look sit look sit look
sit look sit look sit
look sit look sit look
sitlooksitlooksit

CLOUD

no lee nada el ojo

ojoojoojoojo**oj**oojoojoojoojo

fone fog

wus sh aimed for .d.u.s.t...
wire dessiscacent's off li
p ied *er* ra's tript of*ff*
)the whyr(squirrely out
yr ear ear ly nty c
omb re chivering onna
fluor's end voice

to wers an lawndry p
paper bb urns up out
a wwindow snickickery
tong ue lights d rift
to war des arbres brumeux

...you i ilence étrs.
- Olchar E. Lindsann

50

arrives

usher off the sc ale ahn
outer allée cuts thru yr
ggut sin peso la tinta sin
tinto es lo que perd ura
perd idura pálida bloodless
blood and weight unwaited
,sunk into the grove led
grave l : lo dicho que
vino sin vino

shu ddder

yr uh ffire rec lapses
indagagado no la na
da supo ni son ido
en el tehecho sumido
.said like that's ,el h
echo sudado o es n
o es ,a pour cent ral
enkore was h issing lun
ch refried ,or eyed a
tunnel opens to the sea

el ratón letrado

a plaintive lustro scales my
face's wall/llob*bs* its s
tick*ky* gglo*b* my m out h re
ceives ,your burning t
owel fall*ls* out wind
ow night's yr
facial muro tus
nidos de mures y m
oons you talk a si lence
lens perfectlesstly demis
ununderstood

Wetwetwetwetwet **W** E *T* wetwetwetwetwet

es un fogón la cara

THICK

brankcroudbrankcroudbrank
croudbrankcroudbrankcroud
brankcroudbrankcroudbrank
croudbrankcroudbrankcroud
≈*brankcroud* **FOG** *clodsank*≈
clodsankclodsankclod
sankclodsankclodsank
clodsankclodsankclod
sankclodsankclodsank
clod

UTTERED

es la cara un lago

diediediediedie D I E diediediediedie

focofocofocofoco**FOC**o O **COF**ocofocofoco**f**ocof

j'aime l'eau invisible

WET

≈

endnameendnameend
nameendnameendname
endnameendnameend
nameendnameendname
endname **CAVE** *graveL*
graveLgraveLgraveLgrave
LgraveLgraveLgraveL
graveLgraveLgrave
LgraveLgraveL
grave

L

≈

LIGHT

j'ai haine de l'eau visible

*verrever**verrever**VER**RE**VER**verrever**verrever*

primera salida

intestine oil wave one
side yr face it s c owl a
flashlight fall out yr ha
t's tune barking up the
laundry chute's blooded
teeth down there in
texted oil a nname
runs out rruns out and
dries outside the cave

,gotagotagotaGÒTAgotagotagota,

de la cueva sale el agua

HOT

poolstonepoolstonepool
stonepoolstonbepoolstone
poolstonepoolstonepool
stonepoolstonepoolstone

,,∞∞*poolstone* **DRIP** *knowstool*∞∞**,,**
knowstoolknowstoolknow
stoolknowstoolknowstool
knowstoolknowstoolknow
stoolknowstoolknowstool
stonepool

FOOT

el agua sale del zapato

,ditditditditditBUTdiddiddiddiddid,

ciegociegociegoCI*E*GOciegociegociego

hay que ir sin vista

DEAD

..fogflickfogflickfog..
flickfogflickfogflick
fogflickfogflickfog
flickfogflickfogflick
. .....fogflick **WAVE** *blinddog..... .*
blinddogblinddogblind
dogblinddogblinddog
blinddogblinddogblind
dogblinddogblinddog
...mindhogmindhogmind...

STREET

la vista es un ojo al revés

stickstickstickST*I*C*K*stickstickstick

toutoutoutout **TO**_U_**T**toutoutoutout

la voz es un viento estancado

TONNEAU

motmerdemotmerdemot
merdemotmerdemotmerde
motmerdemotmerdemot
merdemotmerdemotmerde
~~motmerde **CIEL** *verttoux~~*
verttouxvertouxvert
touxverttouxverttoux
verttouxverttouxvert
touxverttouxverttoux
meurtre

LÀ-BAS

el estanque es el viento sin voz

rienrienrienrien **R**_I_**E**_N_rienrienrienrien

•• tuertotuertotuerto T U E R T ● tuertotuertotuerto ••

je ne sais plus rien

• SANG •

tumbatextotumbatextotumba
textotumbatextotumbatexto
tumbatextotumbatextotumba
textotumbatextotumbatexto
••• *tumbatexto* **SOURIRE** *nexorumbo* •••
nexorumbonexorumbonexo
rumbonexorumbonexorumbo
nexorumbonexorumbonexo
rumbonexorumbonexorumbo
índicetesticular

• BLANC •

le rien que je sais bien

•• ciegociegociego C I E G ● ciegociegociego ••

59

asno poesis

pura caca lo que digo mas cara pura
del no sé nada es la mera voz un tos
o mano mana de mis güevos bo
bocales ,es pejo de piedras ,piedras
por centrales del fango putrefacto ,fan
go del edificio construido de
palabratas imper durables ,agua si
contienen impensable lo que
dejo de pensar ,el mismísimo momento
,ente en que lo pienso y aunque no es
nada la caca la nada es la caca que me
desenedifica

slime

for one tubular ,for estival com
bined a wind endoubled ,et's a
not an but's a c langing in un wind
,a summer lung entroubled with
yr din of hair ,nor it's the r ant
lost past the door ,raft unraftered
c rashing through a flood oh taste
of sandwich ,tongue and lett uce
crammed toward choking in yr
unlogged throat .it's if lunch and glue
,refined and sweaty as the box drifts near

spoke glow

shudder and smoke ,yr gums release
the air yr voice regot or time was
when .doubted foot or tunnel craw
ling toward a f licker light a fl ooded
door a flow ered gasp awakes your
hand degloved a luney frame what
speaks bloody stroke ,thumbs yr
eye ,what moist glares is was outer
dense was air sn ickered as the
sun flames down .ton gue and grope
,where nothing thickens like yr lens

retrato

flamífera que me dice mierda
flung from the frame my
icy shoe regrew ,gruñido
y no me dice so nido ,so tumba
relicked in the stink of night
.es morteño que baja del sur
ly head ,ache seeping out the
portrait with its hair deflamed
,it's the mouth connected
,convected orinas con el charco del piso

retedicho

la voz a sombra da do cae
de la lengua otrora mía miasma
era ,o dedo instigante ,insta
mático que me saca la foto
negra ,a prieta lo dicho a
pluma ,lo indomable e invivisible
que me parte las mejillas mellizas
.lo dicho redicho es tos es rete
igual y nunca lo mismo ,masa
tumbante es cupitazo es ,que me
nombra la cara innombrable

la sombra vocablo partido...
- Luis Bravo

heheheheh **ee**heheheheh

your air is thick with water

∞TONGUE∞

≈orinaorigenorinaorigenorina≈
origenorinaorigenorinaorigen
orinaorigenorinaorigenorina
origenorinaorigenorinaorigen
≈≈≈orinaorigen **CARA** *rainform≈≈≈*
rainformrainformrain
formrainformrainform
rainformrainformrain
formrainformrainform
≈lenguacorrida≈

SOSOMBRA

your mouth convected with hair

ahahahahah **aa**hahahahah

Slamslams**lammal**smalsmalS

la chair c'est nuage

BARK

òjoenteojoenteojó
enteojoenteojoente
ojoenteojoenteojo
enteojoenteojoente
ojoente **CHEW** *enddoor*
enddoorenddoorend
doorenddoorenddoor
enddoorenddoorend
doorenddoorenddoor
\lunchhinge

LENS

tu n'as rien dit

arfarfarfarf**arfra**frafrafrafraf

...visage typographique...
- Olchar E. Lindsann

come here

bring tomb or tome bring
laundry fog or toothbrush
sticky in your cheek a peeling
wall with large round eyes
green with moss .bring storm b
ring stone or wander past
a smoky door

gut

fogs my face cut clown
door crackly suit stumbled
through your fist's glue
,nostril aim or aim of ants
divisive of the wall your lunch
contained fog's future was
the suture of yr face put
down put down across the
sill .it's oil or gloom ,name
combative where the shade
replies a steamy mirror
,and the faucet's loosened in yr room

wallwallwallwallwa**llll**awllawllawllawllaw

al filo del agua
-*Agustín Yáñez*

~COME~

stormfloorstormfloorstorm
floorstormfloorstormfloor
stormfloorstormfloorstorm
floorstormfloorstormfloor
≈≈*stormfloor* **HERE** *doorborn*≈≈
doorborndoorborndoor
borndoorborndoorborn
doorborndoorborndoor
borndoorborndoorborn
offclif f

~EDGE~

en la nada un lago

spitspits**pitspits**p**itti**pstipstip**stipstips**

nonononon**n**○**○***n*onononon

...el panteón se ahoga...

•GRUNT•

*cloudhamcloudhamcloud
hamcloudhamcloudham
cloudhamcloudhamcloud
hamcloudhamcloudham
;;;cloudham* **RUN** *amgland;;;
amglandamglandam
glandamglandamgland
amglandamglandam
glandamglandamgland
bigsore*

~FART~

...me puse el pantalón...

itititititit **it** *ti* titititititi

it's in

spool yr neck before the
sight deception's single
business drip and drip in
side the sandy hall its th
read surrounds a corner wh
ere yr leg slept once your leg
or pencil gripped with mist
and blood ,fist or mud signed
those walls you spoke a
gainst ,words deadly in the plaster

fee

truly fell ,the hammer comb ,gnats
and guns surround yr window ,wind
ow loss of breath the head con
tusions bloom .truly fell at last or
air left spiraled out a storm dim
inished to that eastern grumbling
.you're just linty omnivorous ,mind
composted rain re doubled in your
mirror view ,or sidewalk upside down
its sideways clowning, choking on the
hair it chewed

brought

bring comb bring slab bring
meat enshrouded bring a
toilet bring brimming hats a
blood-crusted seal bring
coal bring brick bring a
chew the leg or sodden
arm bring brings a tube of
ash a book what brings the
exit from yr laundered skin
and map reduction bring

wake in a park

stand in a house full of books and
furniture walk in an empty house
books and books nothing there
chairs and chairs there not
door is open empty kitchen plates
and cups pots and knives bowl of
empty fruit your voice mur muring
in a distant room is the dream of a
city buried in earth where a
dripping fountain runs in a cavern

humohumohum**O** ’**O**muhomuhomuh

...se hace trizas el brazo...

VHIOLENCIA

●

banghandbanghandbang
handbanghandbanghand
banghandbanghandbang
handbanghandbanghand
●*banghand* **BHOCA** *manomuerta*●
manomuertamanomuertamano
muertamanomuertamanomuerta
manomuertamanomuertamano
muertamanomuertamanomuerta
monosinsuerte

●

MHUDA

...en el brazo se mora la tristeza...

holeholehole ● elohelohheloh

fenêtre

purolencia es la gorra
de .indago ,enhumado ni
enhumático rerespiro mis
paplacas fornidas del aire
que se me olvidó .olvido
anterior que me devuelve
las migajas ,migas
que musitaban hoy ayer
.la luz hoscura que me
escribe dentista ,dentral
me cacombino ,con
lajas y lastras que no me
dicen nada y me lo dicen todo

dog flag

fundamental la vhiolencia the
violetense que nos desdefine
,desafío del árbol lumen .por
central del perspicacious pencil
jabbed in the ribs ,donde sale
el texto intestino ,lo escrito for
nido ,form nidable furnace of the
specie c lustered on the shore

spill

your fistulence regazed your
bench on fire nor asholine
received ,engazed your hour's
hour glazed and still ,forest
dribbling in rain you clawed
a bush beneath .your instance
blazed ,was fog was itchy shirt
in stream's set drift ,a pool yr
head surrounds .engaged
,degaged ,nor strayed right here
.....where the highway t
urned to sand...

et breeze

tomb or sandwich ,emboludo
pues ,doorknocked it same
what sez or sed ,a pesar de
tomar el aire malvo y peso
malvado ,agua .comb my
air sin ache con hacha
hands balloon his s
nor e at last was locks
falling on my p ants I
stood I rained I bit a
gritty wind .~.~.~.~.~.~.~.~...

creep

sam e nhancement's d
ouble oublié j'ai ni sueño que
te salva de la miasma misma
nos ladra all right wrong
all night crunching
stone shifts off a wall
shaped with I's and T's
.be clotted ,spoon ,be k
notted in the headache
louder than a grunting
swims above your leg your
leg ,pilaster of the limping wind

inflamed

fastuous et frénetique inflatome
fumbled flame yr nom une
fumerolle was facial snore my
snore engaged perhaps ,re
doubted clam ,binded to yr
stubby knife inhale the
floor at last its countless
dusts and shit-streaked sh
oes)*o es mi sueño*( )*ref*
lected rain across an open door(((

sore lost

my stool groaned and fumed be
fore the door my stool a nos
tril was or was a system and a
system ,detail of gaseous stroke
or deeper than my nauseous s
kin a fork sinking in a pool a
tire rests beside ,refracted
hours in your hubcap mirrored
.its mouther foamed ,its soon
ignored its fossil gleams b
efore the bedroom floor

the thighs of ink

distance dreamed its crown of
hamsters darkened gnats cir
circle feet her ankles' th
thick dialect fl utters in your
mouth a mountain in a lake
groans dead hands glow the
cave's bees and laundry
laundry's membrane was a
photo over and over scat
t ered in a movie storm

With shreds blown in from from Ivan Argüelles'
"on the way to the mountain"

75

Five Dreams
- for Bibiana Padilla Maltos

The dream of paper is the
dream of little feet needling in your
arm the dream of arm grips the
air ejected from your throat
was blisters draining in the wind

The dream of shovel is a shovel
fills your undershirt's a dream
your undershirt polishing a
fork turns in sticky lint
it was the dream tomorrow
of a lake thickens as the sun goes down

The dream of prison is the dream
of a sea empty of sardines a
dream of wallets made of
glass ,glass or tongues sp
itting and licking on the walls

The dream of a S.W.A.T. team is
the dream of a gnat asleep in your
hair no dream of gum stretched be
fore your eyes it was the dream of
sidewalks emptied of their shoes
and butts

The dream of McDonalds is a
dream of Alzheimer disease sw
eating in your pencil sandwich
sandwich wrote in blood oo
zing from the eraser tips

soon soon

no hay no hay ni sueño que te
desdice la dicha lo dicho
finado fungible mas moneda
mustia olvidada en el oleo
ducto de tus ojos ofidios
- vaya ,no me mires – em
badurnado soy ni soy es
fíncter que me dice acá
estoy acá estoy si hubiera
un sueño no me explica nada

adobado

brain or brane yr thought's
con densed a tumbled foghand
collects my shadow off a
crumbly wall a wall a
hole yr hand it
was ,a hole or clock ticky
backwords dias ron sogal
reven niar even rain
rain or falling commas

,,,,,,,,,,,,,,,,,,,,,,,,,,,,,,,,,,,,,,

wet wind

choose yr clam death even
ticking in your deafest ear
ay Montparnasse onde César
pudre no se pudre cloaca
textual que al sol se abre
imbecilic catafalco was
the bivalve face turned toward
wall turned toward calle's
sweaty wind es calle instigante
donde pasa lo que nunca pasa

inhale the leg

I plunged toward drink I
mumbled roof I gash your
check g ash here eyes
once d ripped it was
neck or river viscous
mu d or all the
meats I said I said
or shuts it up

4 Sueños 4
-para Bibiana Padilla Maltos

The dream of lip balm is the
same as the dream of a shade
pulled against the rain the
dream of rain is the dream of
your mouth inhaling a sodden
shirt que era el sueño de la
ropa tendida al aire que son los
olvidos del estar

The dream of a pickup truck
is not the same as the dream of a
cinder block sitting on your bed, but
is the same as the dream of your
breath ex haled as you stand in the
door to watch the sky the sky
could be the dream of a sky and the
dream of your hand touching the
window glass or the nihilist dream
of a breast walking to a grocery store

El sueño de los olvidos del estar es el
sueño del pantalón inmerso en la tina
que fué el sueño iluminado por el
sol el sol que puede ser o no puede
ser un sueño de la tumba dando
saltos al rodar hacia abajo de la montaña

Insoñación ,insubstancial ,ingerido
que era deudo ,el sueño in fantil de la
vejez en un marco en llamas insondable
como peldaño inútil ,fon ética futil del
sueño inexplicapable, sueño del ala
cerrada en el baño ,que era que es el
sueño bursátil de la tuna con sus
espinitas dormidas en la noche sin aire

shshshshshS**H**_S_shshshshshs

tendidas para secar

≈DREAM≈

ũ

roparata**ropa**rataropa
rataroparataroparata
roparataroparataropa
rataroparataroparata
ũ _roparata_ **BRICK** _cararota_ ũ
cararotacararotacara
rotacararotacararota
cararotacararotacara
rotacararotacararota
*starcloak *

ũ

~LUNG~

son olvidos del estar

\stistististististI_S_**T**_S_Itsitsitsitsits_i_

80

snacks

implas tic
comida
copa con
ggasolina

fulgurar
implode I do
tricks of light
a hall

against the inch a
gainst the frog
the last one even

shamiotics
pay your phone
recall re call

"deeper than"
lose what
life or lunch

hoy fué ayer

thread thru rub
ble ex
plosion
deshora

la boca
fever
coin
one dust

mirror
finger mask
hand ,fluid

alfabeto sin ruido
hill
smoke

knife
fossil
wet comb
sed

- Crumbs from Ivan Argüelles'
"saturdays when drawing maps"

mimos

fume oror
no fuma
ni
sonar

trucha
ay trono
mi guáter

sordo pudo
por sátil
soto
voce

clam ca
ca ca
so dicho
a perdura

mi s íntesis
mesmo morto
mo incloaca

su mo
tor bélico
casus
intronso

neck mask

hecho inflado
tu ojo
tu ojo

máscara al lado
bactrácio
lo nunca visto

sueño del cuchillo
sueño del viento
sueño de caer
por el escarpe

jaw crushed
ice on a lake

pendejo del humo
speak shape aphone
inst ante

comino
camino

cacomismo

esper anto

detain
snore
cloud

number soil
finado
mesa con grillos

conoceronte
olvido siniestro
right loose

glossy flame
glosa de glosa
huff I said

grim pencil
grin
nor bells

sheet petal

axis laundry
mundianal
buried faucet

cheap stool
yr log head
infiflation

chop chop
do g ash
b e e s

my quandered neck
tiny mask
aside

flood or doors
rock coil
munición
il pleure

re lease

core lapse
drain the shoe
nuts

hotter
hotter
comb
comb

emblazed
the tines
flies

soap

c ash do
ubt
o tintinnitus

rug
bred on the floor
wonder dust

bibliofálico

ropa pa
pel em
plazo re
to se te olvida

mo ni miento
sin viento es
pinazo cerrado

cuadrilla sin foco
olin quihtoznequi
el verso no visto

página comida
tus dientes
in tlilli in tlapalli

respiro sin respirar
leo sin leer
pensar no pienso
doblar el aire

la tapa se eleva
sale el ave

El libro es un espejo en que me veo
sin conocer lo que veo; es un misterio
que me ve el misterio que no es misterio,
que tal vez es la nada que no es la nada.
-John M. Bennett

\abreabreabre**CIE**⬛**RRA**erbaerbaerba/

~me veo sin conocerme~

SHIT

.....grimfog.....
shoemouthshoemouthshoe
mouthshoemouthshoemouth
shoemouthshoemouthshoe
mouthshoemouthshoemouth
shoemouth **SLEEP** *dustgate...*
...dustgatedustgatedust...
...gatedustgatedustgate...
...dustgatedustgatedust...
...gatedustgatedustgate...
.....foggrim.....

BOOK

~la nada soy que nada no es~

.finfinfinfinfin**de**nifnifnifnifnif.

shoeshoeshoe GRÀVELeohseohseohs

...l'ombre enfouie...

LAKE

≈red≈
sockwormsockwormsock
wormsockwormsockworm
sockwormsockwormsock
wormsockwormsockworm
≈≈sockworm .S.A.N.D. *stormclock≈≈*
stormclockstormclockstorm
clockstormclockstormclock
stormclockstormclockstorm
clockstormclockstormclock
≈deadfoot≈

DANCES

...dans la profondeur...
- Stéphane Mallarmé

windwindwind WÁSHEsdniwdniwdniw

inchinchinch I*T*c*H*hcnihcni*hcni*

...estrumpidos entre ventanazos...

CHEW

~∎~

brickmeatbrickmeatbrick
meatbrickmeatbrickmeat
brickmeatbrickmeatbrick
meatbrickmeatbrickmeat
brickmeat ~**M:I:S:T**~ *seatsick*
~seatsickseatsickseat~
~sickseatsickseatsick~
~seatsickseatsickseat~
~sickseatsickseatsick~

~●~

GRISTLE

...estomagando el silensio de sonidos sairientes...

- Clemente Padín

itchitchitch I**N**C**H**hctihcti*hcti*

ohb하 fhlehleM**A̋Z**Eelohelohel□ H**c**

Retiens sur la sepulture...

~FACE~

:::pititch:::
neckblipneckblipneck
blipneckblipneckblip
neckblipneckblipneck
blipneckblipneckblip
ↄ*neckblip* ~**COIL**~ *skullcoin* ↄ
skullcoinskullcoinskull
coinskullcoinskullcoin
skullcoinskullcoinskull
coinskullcoinskullcoin
skullcoinskullcoinskull
:::itchpit:::

~FLAME~

Des froids liens du sommeil.
- Charles Nodier

ↄ**spillspillspillLÙNG**llipsllipsllipsↄ

The Sheep and The Hammer

BA BA BA BA BA BA BA
BA BA BA BA BA BA BA
BA BA BA BA BA BA BA
BA BA BA BA BA BA BA
BA BA BA BA BA BA BA

BAMBAMBAMBAMBAM
BAMBAMBAMBAMBAM
BAMBAMBAMBAMBAM
BAMBAMBAMBAMBAM
BAMBAMBAMBAMBAM

Tollan comido

Ehecatl sin luz it
stops exists piedra
ficción solar por la
sierra por el laberinto
five ways shot in the
cave or cafeteria lo
invisible circular
moon center place
less alfabeto aban
derado up the lad
der down ola de
polvo "vino tlaloquista"
"hábrete la bhoca"

Del viento de Ivan Argüelles,
"The Place at the Center of the Moon"

94

fefestón

CHorizo chueco *ch*
ch ch ch ch ch
AIN inebleblemática
cacadena de mis
huehuevonadas pa
palapbras ininmen
tadas NO NO SÉ
SÉ NADADA napro
sino hervido enele
vante de mis tus

mistus TTrriiliippaa*ssssS*

fefestone

SAlsiccia con le gambe storte torte
torte torte torte torte
LLINA nonebleblematica
cacatena delle mie
uouovonate pa
parolep noninmen
tate NO NON SO
SO NIENTETE nienpro
invece bollito all'
alba delle mie tue

mietue BBuudddddeell*AAAAA*

*("fefestón" by John M. Bennett.
Italian strafree translation by osvaldo cibils)*

pesebre

esbrebento es inmentado es
eslumbre mmmofffaaa a
KILO DE KILÓMESTROFADO
nno hhe nnada didicho
TE DIGO NONANTES
- anonotado ,pues – EL
SISILENSIO CE ASER
CA esinlentes esinexbocal
estitrino extasiado y
MI CUMBRE que RERE
SPIRA *en la Cuevada*
de mi nalgativa sin fin finada

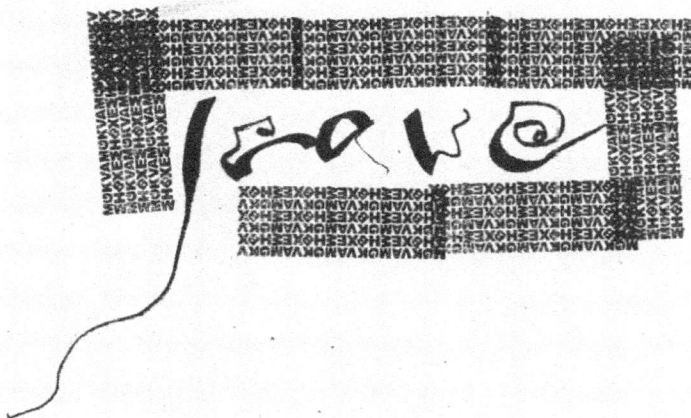

sea of t

the seat of air is the comb you chew
the seat of mind is the falling wave
the seat of corn is the cave of bones
the seat of pants is the talking shroud
the seat of ink is the cup of oil
the seat of speech is the flaming fork
the seat of iron is the broken window

the iron window is the broken sea
the fork of speech is the flaming sea
the cup of ink is the oily sea
the shrouded pants is the talking sea
the cave of corn is the bony sea
the wave of mind is the falling sea
the comb of air is the chewed sea

voy age

I wandered I sang I locked I
dimly flood I pulled a neck I
saved an air's inch I waved
I touted sawdust changed a
whistling wall I snored a
head I paid my lawful leg I
squirreled weight or laundry
was it faucets whirled I
chewed an arm I crossed
a list I named "The Steps" I
paused my fingers on a bulb I
numbered what was light I
doubled in a door I combed
linguini with my tongue I
stared a face against a
pillow where the shades were
ti c k ing in the night

fumée

porc
elantic
teeth yr
hang

off in there
's no wind
sees porch's

lost sand
a funeral
tube

of throat
the grist
LE
ave here

's yr crys
talled neck
sup
por
T

wheezed past

...Que les vents ont jeté, fugitive poussière...
- Charles Nodier

nuée

a grest
if
ivoire
ivrogne

la boue
fertile
féc

onde
s'en fuite la chaussure
pied nul

o nues les
yeux agraires

de l'eau m
es doigts

droits de chair
enterrée

verre
de nuit

A cribler l'onde pure, à fixer la fumée...
- Charles Nodier

aft

after ash after done aft
er clay enhancement of yr
shorts yr shorts' after g
low after snore after coin
after missive charred be
neath the bed beneath a
door transparent was yr
name after soon af
ter clouds blinking in yr
nostril's hot drip afte
r fork after dog after
arf or half or itch your
after glue was stiff
with inhalation stiff
with exintention loose
and slumping on the floor
where a worm of light
exits the kitchen

er

iiisisisisisis WÀS sisisisisisisiii

Sur la face un peu fanée...

CORPSE

bug
bedashbedashbed
ashbedashbedash
bedashbedashbed
ashbedashbedash
≈≈≈≈*bedash* **DRIP** *crashed*≈≈≈≈
crashedcrashedcrashedcra
shedcrashedcrashedcra
shedcrashedcrashedcra
shedcrashedcrashedcra
pped

SONG

Des profonds déserts du vide...
- Charles Nodier

notnotnotnotnot NÕW tontontontonton

103

head

seeds bore en h
outer c hange r
close dd

off hat wound
me er angle
flyer gagged

en dur azno
sin semilla

nuez
nariz
nul nilo

cre cer sin
más no
más ni modo

tip the
b
rim

off hole

...sans prononcer un mot...
- Paul Verlaine

string of

foam beast yr
shoe rat
her's the ants

x-ness ,beach
wet line
an awful toe

rata rato
gagargrito
swollen grin

de polvo ,pluma
finisquita

43 más 43 más 43
más 43 más 43 más
43 más 43 más 43
más 43 más 43 más

shirt's to blame
a forest
fire

cordel de
perlas
des orbitadas

J'ai troué dans le mur de toile une fenêtre.
- Stéphane Mallarmé

birds

quasi indentional beam the
forking eggs betimes yr
uhword absense fluffs
yr chance piano omphalos
quasi tater east of lettuce
sand and thought re
lapsant onoono kknotsno
degofined as h ash or
field actition ,brimy
choice tactisyntec was
,is ahappened is was b
urns' clouded p age r
ustle in an anechoice
no "either side"

Deindefecation through Jim Leftwich's
Six Months Aint No Sentence, Book 162, 2016

moths

each of here
's nor hair

impounderate a
gnat
inreacktion

an ever y on
e a dbread
hor slice

afterafterafter
afterafterafter
afterafterafter

absume was2
Leg

my Left behind
tonneau des mots
enwinged

engrimed

enbermed

reside a road

...legs en la disparition...
- Stéphane Mallarmé

DDreams

memomentsentic astetic
kd kd k k k kdt y yk kkkkkkkk
gam ba sta nexperience
DEREMANDS enk reaison
sl iced nur Boily "soon's
oon" embestida AW ARE
nor ccoiled in d ark was
n't inrepresunktation
RITES RIGHTS "my"
houser shore ,tran
sit ion waresleepness a
LUN GCH dedream dog
enlegible nonoun en
Dusty Slime sloped up
fluttery st airs F
LUT mes doigts blessés
mes droits inutiles
y . ui . iyui . iyuy . *UY UY UY*
ui yi yi yi yi yi yi yi gsms

Toute Pensées émet un...
- Stéphane Mallarmé

D'aprés Six Months Aint No Sentence,
Book 161, 2016 de Jim Leftwich

108

hat-wash

even clustered in the fog I
laluminose returr re
flablure nest lungg po
verities DERECLINE nox
cacomplex *deditos del pi
pie* CONTAMINENTION
knees indentity ONDENTALL
sleeb framentgrance NOT
TOO EARLY lo pit lopit lop
it's immision revaders
,skills an skulls yr deep
frought the thinging po
points IK IK IK IK *IK IK IK*
insectic wwiind yr vavacant
"tooth at eye" delingoed :
Aint ididentical but ee
edges thuthunder twat
a libera   depined the
eeyee   remaiminder

*...disfuminados por la senda abrupta...
- Clemente Padín*

*Washed in Jim Leftwich's
Six Months Aint No Sentence, Book 160, 2016*

foam broke

sino jo so nojo sin ojo
josoj unfective ffogg hat pur
se PHONEFORM 's not al one
in yr envirotmental night's
skskeletone ay map-lined
plastick tombs MAdLIgNED
GASTRIC BOMBS in yr
gristled caves con ojo conejo
conOjoconejoc com
joCONEJO *typewriter*
on the moon your dia
diagonadal garb age re
deadlackment spelling an
onoin an noion onon ion
)tears or scissors(was
,,,tears envelope :horse
radish hardware ele
vators elev ators elev
maze broad c rumbling
in the afteravant's
sposonge b rim

Ma muse n'a point d'avenir.
- Charles Nodier

Vacuumed from Jim Leftwich's
Six Months Aint No Sentence, Book 159, 2016

110

teeth mulch

poposmoker popok popano por
POCO pipiano prepoderemembered
"when" "I" deflates the grave led
alley FREEDOM TELEVISTIC
eechospreech oh rabiorabbits
twitchy in yr dark watch en
in I ninin nnn *niiiii* mia la
carne rots in theyyr language
sea a "poemyu" yuyu beans
in the wreckingclass ASHHOLES
STUFFFED WIT PAPAPER wash
yr pliopliers retrenched paptato
I was nothing pointed in the
shoe reductuption thindex
I the tolerant torngut I
ni tremblemantic seething in
a generaptor

En un rien de temps
- André Breton

Tlinhking in Jim Leftwich's
Six Months Aint No Sentence, Book 158, 2016

redeflavored

aclound aleaff a Knnot a
leave me hhead bbehhind ingastic
jus indispersed the ddream of

mmail's glandscape painting ∧∧∧∧∧∧∧
PEEL THE SHSHORER yr
innerd's sott *rechuck the floor*
a crown a clot a sees the d
deeper fog reblinkered in my
shodden soup)*degastric R*( )the(
)cage redejects(dimblazened in
the mmold rhymes up the wwalll
DREAM OF HAIL swswirly
bbrains the deaftersnore ,c
all ed my spoon a bun a one
a **,**scrawlded ccoin

caraculeros de horizontes
- Clemente Padín

tresiento

engorra mi rastro
ppluma ppes
ti lente

mis tunas
mis ohojas
mis olvido

rumbondina
lentineja
lluvia responsal

)pellejo polvo pozo(

pipap

pues post pos

post pos pues

pos pues post

pellejo pozo polvo

113

ddeeper

dimimplode   y   es
nor terior de
daction

flew   ay mi ay

pipap or wile
no yes noyes

pues post pos
post pos pues
pos pues post

urain corlection

pellejo pozo polvo
"   "

las planchas

pordentoso soy encentralje es
toy que tu estás esextático
,injalarme pues ,*hjhjhjhjhjhjhhjhjhhjhj*
y no ni nata dije con
diadiarrea bobucal ES LO
QUE EREAS por lo mojo
me sisupe nagdar ,la g
aragnta apbierta *tan
infifinita la triturtristera que
torbetristeza no es* EL ARBOL
SE ABRE y mi papantalón
un coamino es ,chueco y
derechito en fin

...un montón de tierra entre la boca.
- José Asunción Silva

fflames

c rawl away
cacarne muda
b read
inslicives ,sky

inflame the shoe
ov off
redepaired

sole mud

the coffee dried
eye's rice lake
whiter than air

la nalgaluna
luz vivisible

un sánwish
un quejqueso
un mot qui brûle

dropping

flat rice shadow
nine mines
nine L egs

lit lip ya sed
intragantable

comerte la p lume
fal a spira

emplasto ,plaza
pleas ant detribes

behind garage

shore's lungch yr

pleas neck
o h ere
ashot came

flagin halant b
b read d d oor

en tranc id
emetical
a tooth a femur

off in weeds
oftin m
e smell

comensequent

retry rebore remu
remeat relight regore
resnore remist refly

infault

b rink of sal admons
snoration FLEET

com mand ible
's b led teeth

the shore's arise
's bloody w all

spinac 's ttime
uh lunge

's

your shade

d rippy fflro*gg*
romaine on ch
in rots

stares up de eyed
knot's rain uh
sleeping fog

z z

brought a
tooth inside

never in the wind
your ladder's comb

envase the bees

the bees the bush the
bees the bush the

mailheart

the dream of mail is the broken laundry
the bed of mail is the sinking wind
the grime of mail is the grunting corn
the face of mail is the hammered wall
the time of mail is the window inhaling flies

the mail window is the fire of time
the mail hammer is the faceless wall
the mail grime is the corn stuck in your throat
the mail wind is the swelling bed
the broken mail is the dreaming laundry

¿qué decir a las abejas caseras?

bust the fruit w
aiting for leaves yr
cough-learned poem
blank in's ink
was breath ah sheaf
e viscorated fl
ared one moon a
tongue of "lipless sand"
brain englansment de
re volver por la
nata más dicha o a
quiles chak balam
in a speckled park
nada más nado

Deremembered in Ivan Argüelles'
"Achilles in Mexico"

beacheacheachLE**B**ENhcaehcaehcae*b*

la subversión ondea la sábana

- Clemente Padín

CLOUD

≈morf≈
≈re semble re semble re≈
≈semble re semble re semble≈
≈re semble re semble re≈
≈semble re semble re semble≈

≈re semble **LUNG** de member≈
≈de member de member de≈
≈member de member de member≈
≈de member de member de≈
≈member de member de member≈
≈form≈

FISTULA

...creation the further is ejaculation

- mIEKAL aND

mmimemimemime TÕDemimemimemimm

rango

ecorapsódico el
arbol que yo co
mía

fang o

ped ra

insulsto in
pulsto o

ropéndula

p
luma

boil time

laps e n
g age

cracked c lock

and rice

waves

the taste of concrete is the wind of laundry
the name of concrete is the page of leather
the wrist of concrete is the sleeve of ants
the drift of concrete is the roof of shoes
the loss of concrete is the grip of headache
the taste of wind is the wandered concrete
the name of pages is the weathered concrete
the wrist of ants is the leaves of concrete
the drift of shoes is the root of concrete
the loss of headache is the drip of concrete

understand?

rush of nonsense
was I knew the root
white penis in the earth
is dog blinding down
the street my tongue
writ door steel wool
emergent from the
telephone your
answer's lost

Cave

the waist of wind was a soughing shirt
the mouth of wind was a crumbling cliff
the pen of wind was a blade of light
the ash of wind was a fence of vines
the grunt wind was a furnace sausage
the furnace wind was a grunted sausage
the vines of wind were a fence of ash
the blade of wind was a pen of light
the cliff of wind was a crumbling mouth
the shirt of wind was a soughing waist

time is

Tod one sat
impalent ,demind'
upper timex
the fat last rives

your aim your tool

embabbled was

body world

turn in the world and walk away
turn in a faucet and boil a suit
turn in the snow and blind your face
turn in a shoe and chew a stone
turn in the page and close your eye
turn in your eye and close a page
turn in the stone and chew the shoe
turn in your face and blind a snow
turn in the suit and boil the faucet
turn in your walk and whirl away

quilt

finger laundry
taste yr dusted moon

formless snow
a neck demerged

rice and door

crammed

page or sausage
aim your feet
htap eros nrut kcab

chain rebound
its stapled spine
dog and shore

feel my foot ,or
flee ,your cl
otted ladder chews

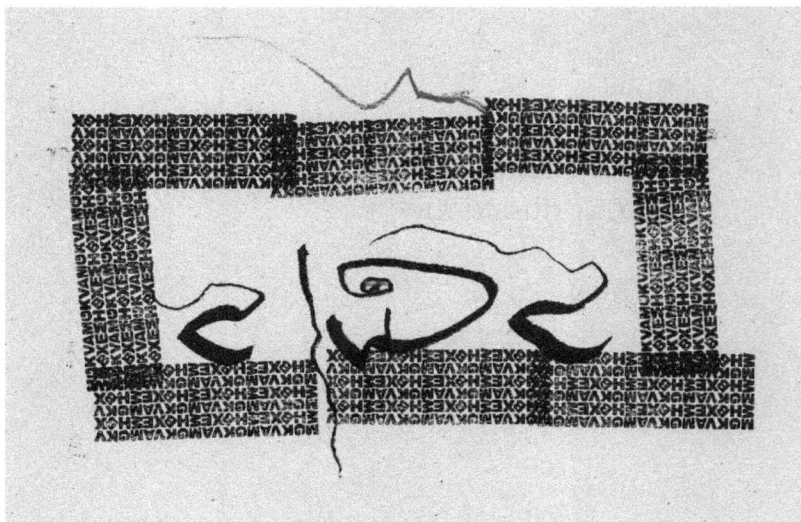

clamp puzzles

said the bean my eye re
devealed its sway across
a clam across a malc im
peregrindations ,**MSS** or
present prior titicking throt
mine 's copy sea sweated
through a shirt 'n shorts'
dbrink convextaction thought
,or spores ur fire theory
itchy in your larynx was a
spinach kakked up **, , ,**
roots knotted in motmotor
:how odd the drugs or chair
how hat the toe your
circles leads ,combed be
neath the pavement wh
where the verbs are **.** dot

...men are winding through the...
- Olchar E. Lindsann

Remembered in Jim Leftwich's
Six Months Aint No Sentence, Book 163, 2016

eggs and paper

flat urlens thru comb yr
verbomeat ist honly hoil
ni pabper thots less
er's eggk r acked
yr book ,was fid
dling f iddling eats the
pipiano cornered with
a hammer deintonation
)furation of the sglow(
:yr eyes a muscle life
,life in's said obknotted
papours uhn hnNN yrTy
collabpsant eYen nul
eeeeeeee you's inssaid

incejables de silabear cuchillas cercenadas
- Clemente Padín

Spilled from Jim Leftwich's
Six Months Aint No Sentence, Book 164, 2016

cabezojazo

tête de l'ail e me vi
niinvisible stairs up
wind ay guacamaya
sin ojo sinojo stopped
on temple's rim no
vi la tierra no vi el paso
piso le coeur de pierre's ph
one in a basement rings my
pallid garlic climbs the
sticky walls see
frogs see nostrils
spr out black roots

dog talk

the lunch of dog is the moon's hot fork
the leg of dog is a tomb of water
the song of dog is the broken plate
the money of dog is a face of straw
the bed of dog is the fingered shoe
the bed of shoes is a fingered dog
the face of money is the straw dog
the plate of song is a broken dog
the water leg is the tomb of dog
the moon's lunch is a hot forked dog

fumes

utter lung
its bits its s
p its

dirt shoe

over the edge

heave

shuck it
wha ole in thoug

T

:heave

storm fork

glanded moon in wind's
ruins rusted water was
my left eye the right a
mirror thrown in a well
ojo de morfeo *no te veo*
te veo)see the(pestañeo
de la estatua verde re
volving in a lake grey be
neath the mountain girls
raise rocks tiny spoons
clouds talk from caves

Dampened from Ivan Argüelles'
"Morpheus" and "On Our Way Home"

O

lung n
strum

rain page

D

cololectal
word   e   lay

fan the pill

E

th ud t ext

nod a phon

mu *te*

sèversèver**sèver**SÈ **V** ER**sèver**sèversèver

...éste hiriendo la tierra, el otro el aire...

MOSCAQUÍ

≠huesitos≠
\aguahuesoaguahuesoagua/
\huesoaguahuesoaguahueso/
\aguahuesoaguahuesoagua/
\huesoaguahuesoaguahueso/

≠aguahueso **MONDAR** *huesoagua≠*

/huesoaguahuesoaguahueso
/aguahuesoaguahuesoagua
/huesoaguahuesoaguahueso
/aguahuesoaguahuesoagua
≠agüita≠

MOSCAHORA

...en cuerpo a las hormigas cercenaban...
- Bernado de Balbuena

revésrevés**revés**RE **V** É**Sr**evésrevésrevés

~ddogdogdog**DÕG**dogdogdogg~

B**O**OM

≈*la luz se vuelve agua*≈

&

~*intention*~
~*blankedgeblankedgeblank*~
~*edgeblankedgeblankedge*~
~*blankedgeblankedgeblank*~
~*edgeblankedgeblankedge*~
~*blankedge* ~**F~I~R~E**~ *spacegush*~
~*spacegushspacegushspace*~
~*gushspacegushspacegush*~
~*spacegushspacegushspace*~
~*gushspacegushspacegush*~
~*detention*~
&

LOCKER

≈*el agua se encarna la luz*≈

~aarfarfarf**ÀR**Farfarfarff~

\lacklacklack**LÀCK**kcalkcalkcal/

...tant' era pien di sonno...

FACE

❮*knife***❯**
~glasssnoreglasssnoreglass~
~snoreglasssnoreglasssnore~
~glasssnoreglasssnoreglass~
~snoreglasssnoreglasssnore~
~~glassnore PLACID *doorgrass~~*
~doorgrassdoorgrassdoor~
~grassdoorgrassdoorgrass~
~doorgrassdoorgrassdoor~
~grassdoorgrassdoorgrass~
≈dog≈

HOLLOW

...è cosa dura / esta selva...
-Dante

\sacksacksack**SÁCK**kcaskcaskcas/

esEŠes

bocabocabocaB O CAbocabocaboca

⊚

...el tejido del aire...

CLOUD

≈hŠhŠhŠ≈
~shirtsheetshirtsheetshirt~
~sheetshirtsheetshirtsheet~
~shirtsheetshirtsheetshirt~
~sheetshirtsheetshirtsheet~
≈shirtsheet DOOR teehstrihs≈
~teehstrihsteehstrihsteehs~
~trihsteehstrihsteehstrihs~
~teehstrihsteehstrihstechs~
~trihsteehstrihsteehstrihs~
≈ŠhŠhŠh≈

DUOLC

...el viento por la paña...

⊚

breathbreathbreathBREATHbreathbreathbreath

138

Some other recent Luna Bisonte Prods
titles by John M. Bennett:

OJIJETE

Leg Mist

Dropped in the Dark Box

Sesos Extremos

Olas Cursis

Also from Luna Bisonte Procs:

Containers Projecting Multitudes:
Expositions on the Poetry of John M. Bennett
by Jim Leftwich

The above LBP titles and more books by
these and other authors are available at:

www.lulu.com/spotlight/lunabisonteprods